a crash of rhinos

This book was supported by
a grant from the Greenwall Fund
of The Academy of American Poets

paisley rekdal

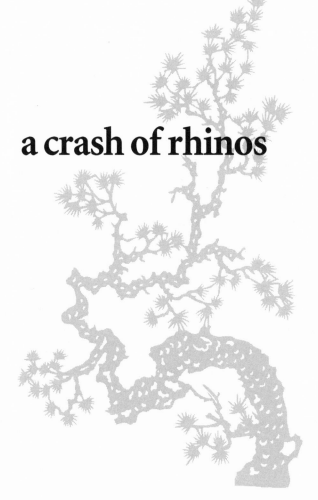

a crash of rhinos

THE UNIVERSITY OF GEORGIA PRESS   ATHENS & LONDON

Published by the University of Georgia Press
Athens, Georgia 30602
© 2000 by Paisley Rekdal

Designed by Erin Kirk New
Set in 10 on 15 Minion
Printed and bound by McNaughton & Gunn

The paper in this book meets the guidelines for
permanence and durability of the Committee on
Production Guidelines for Book Longevity of the
Council on Library Resources.

Printed in the United States of America
04   03   02   01   00   P   5   4   3   2   1

Library of Congress Cataloging-in-Publication Data

Rekdal, Paisley.
A crash of rhinos / Paisley Rekdal.
p.   cm.
ISBN 0-8203-2273-3 (pbk. : alk. paper)
I. Title
PS3568.E54 C73 2000
811'.6—dc21   00-044730

British Library Cataloging-in-Publication Data available

for eric

contents

acknowledgments

The Asian Pacific American Journal: "Captain Cook Discovers Tattooing,"
    an excerpt
Crab Orchard Review: "Joe Louis and the War Effort, or How My
    Grandfather Acquired the Laundromat"
Crazyhorse: "Fire"
Earth's Daughters: "Crescent Down Works Factory"
Poetry Motel: "Love Phones"
The Sonora Review: "The History of the Slow Dance"
Willow Springs: "Night Sweeper"

"A Crash of Rhinos" and "Captain Cook Discovers Tattooing" appeared
in the anthology *Starting Rumors: America's Next Generation of Writers* by
Mesa State Press, 1999.

"Night Sweeper" is for Al Richardson, the manager of Forest Plaza.

"Drink Me" is for Christa MacAuliff, the schoolteacher who died in the
Challenger Shuttle explosion.

"Fire" is for my parents.

"Making Out in Korean" is based on an international "dating" reference
book by the same title. Italicized lines are some of the phrases included in
the original.

Thanks to David Baker, Thylias Moss, Raymond McDaniel, Cathy Carlisi,
Susan Brown, Adrian Fillion, Eric Heimann and my parents.

a crash of rhinos

As when the station's engineer pops the hood
of our radio board to change time and it is as surprising
as the complicated weather keeping us indoors all day,
so the liver is more intelligent
than the man, the common gut muscle better trained than a policeman's
German Shepherd. Just as we know gain
is often its own sacrifice, as when we read of the political
prisoner on Robben Island suddenly turning
to poems for survival, who saved his daily sheets of toilet paper
for a few words to be crammed inside his bed, so cruelty —
teaches purpose, though perverted.   —
We know we could destroy the organ with attention.
And so of holistic self-measurement of blood pressure, a rat's
decision between sex or food: the autonomy of interior
domain we have opened to new question. Ghost in the machine,
divine spark? For soul itself read "choice." We know bodies
provide their needs and directions, as when the corpus politic
sections off to voting blocks, the tropic bird has brooding patches
grown to transmit heat from belly to egg, and the lumens
of our vessels are gently lavaged through with blood. "Adaptation"
means conscious wrestling with life, the daily amazement
of us. We've heard psychologists conclude that organs can benefit
from operant conditioning, stones from kidneys thrown
from the visceral loop through deep-breathing exercises,
brain waves at will rewritten like simple scores of notes
in a measure. Just so, we ask for things we cannot know.
We beg skin shed, the sky inhale a lake for rain
because we trust; because even tiny events are political
and there's work so simple that to do it would exhaust us.
We should be no more than occasional
engineers come to prop the board, adjust the clock, heal
when healing is possible. Just so, praise
for the mandrill's snout, the booby's blue, startling
feet. It is courage we ask of each other now. Courage
and the freedom faith and inattention make possible.

Nature would provide the models: solar cells styled from juniper leaves, steel fibers woven spider-style, shatterproof ceramics drawn from mother-of-pearl.

I

a crash of rhinos

What's your pet name? Collective noun?
What will Snookums do today? Your bedmate
pulls quarters magically from behind your ear, one
for each hour you've spent together. When he stops
there's fifty cents sliding into the sheets and his tongue
covering the pink cauliflower of your nipple. "Beautiful
defects," he whispers into your body. "Ah, Nature." Roll away,
don't care when he calls you "Thumper." By noon you'll be
nose to nose anyway, a sloth of bears, snoozing
your way into this relationship.

Ah, Nature. You could tell him its startling fact
is not its defects but its sameness. A uniformity
suggestive of some single-cell prototype, our Adam/Eve
genome plucked, as scientists think, from the thread
of a lightning bolt. Darling, today you're more
than anonymous, one sexy blip among the thousand
couples grunting in each other's arms; defined by Loving,
your action. Flying geese only recognized
by the form they make in the sky.
A crash of rhinos, piece of asses. Stinkhead:
everything comes in boring droves of hogs.

This is how you got here. Mid-morning he tallies your union
in terms of snakes, tarantulas, the evolutionary needs
of common flagellates till you scorn science: its primal
urge to pair like scared cows shoved ass to ass in circles
for defense. A clutch of penises! What is love but fear?

That soft storm at your periphery, sudden hand
pushing you below surface? Thoughts, as you age or sicken,
sifted from consciousness like dusts of starlings: Love me,
little lamb. No one should die alone.

Sweetheart, all your friends are married.
Packs of teazles? Kerfs of panters? A multiplicity of spouses.
Today only two quarters protect you
from loneliness. It's out of your hands. The job
didn't pan, checks bounce, 2 A.M. is its own
worst child. This is your last magic trick.
"Kumquat," he whispers. Lover. Loved one.
And the soul begs always, *Leave me leave me*
while the body says simply, *Stay.*

the history of the slow dance

Husband #4 taught me to dance in church, back
inside those yellow rooms where they served coffee. Primped,
white, age 13: my classmates and I bandaged every corner
like a wound. We noted handfuls of pink husbands starched
off their sofas Saturday night—teachers' spouses,
each a congregation of flustered goodwill. Mine
pressed me flat to shirtfront where an unending reel
of dinner spooled behind his buttons.
It was the Romantics. "El Choclo," "Cherry Pink
and Apple White." The instructor had jerry-rigged
this scene for a waltz but my Husband didn't know it
so we shuffled in each other's clutch till time was called.
I remember it as my first obscenity come to life: soft nub
of the man's scalp gleaming in the urine-toned light
as he bent to offer me compliments. I, realizing,
as I took them, something in me was finally old enough
to fake gratitude.
                    "Hustle" is the Dutch word
for "shake," known underground as the quick stumble
of the victim whose pockets get picked. In the '70s
Puerto Rican girls lined the bars in Queens to dance it first,
twisting a little at the hip in their partners' arms.
Those tender, neon moves Travolta made
famous. But slow dancing isn't really
the hustle; it's no botched waltz or bossa
nova, no subtle movement, as a critic might say,
of our interior stage. Still, it is the landscape we know best. Space
after the stereo's ground to its stale halt, the moves
left after the vodka has taken its toll. People,
you know, have since held me closer

than the Husband, that dim historic bald spot. Fly
to fly, extrusive asses clutched tight in each other's hands
like grenades we might just drop: these
are a few early gestures forgotten in my slouch
toward now. I'd like to think, standing in the shade
of church where neon Jesus lights the way back to Roosevelt,
that girl stumbling from her velvet corridor knows a little
of the history departed from us; bone-deep
how what threatens can be so tender, those urges
we've since let drop away like sequin sprays,
the crow's foot of a false eyelash. And she'll show us
simply by walking into the light. There,
that way, in the body slumped and insignificant. Her face
so vandalized, it must reveal everything.

love phones

1. The Problem

"ok so I'm a lesbian," begins tonight's show
and it's Caitlin worried that her girlfriend now likes men
but won't come out. "Beautiful," moans the intern
as the certified-sex-therapist–cum–show host giggles
in the mic. They've got solid radio
format: good host/bad host. Dr. Judy's sweet while Jagger
sneers at gay men and adolescents. So

"I don't get," says the third girl this evening,
"why my boyfriend stops talking after we have sex,"
and it's Jagger's turn: "Because you're dull."
After two hours of this, it's true—everyone's
dull. Even the mother caught at the neighborhood orgy
by her 17-year-old, the boy who masturbates in the county abattoir,
the wife who wakes each day with sperm
lacing her face. It's understood

the advice is meant to be educational
for those neophytes of love, the public school sex
    -ed flunkees whose already watered understanding
of sex consists solely of having gotten pregnant; Aphrodite's
least learned, most deprived, or simply dumbest
percentage of America's population. "Well, Caitlin,"

Judy purrs, "What is it about your girlfriend's attraction
to men that bothers you?" *Beep.*
Jagger disconnects the line the second she stammers.
By 11:10 the usual has happened:

some earnest fan calls in to chastise him for thoughtlessness.
Just what does he do besides harass? Jagger plays up rage.
"Are you getting wood there?" he spits.
"Does this sort of thing turn you on, you pimple,
you ass . . ." Mid-sentence the satellite

transmission's switched. The station is back
to rock format till 2 A.M. while we, insistently
disinterested, drift along in bed.
Up to our necks in today's dishes and work, garbage still
swaddled in sacks. The argument dangles mid-air.
We have to wait till tomorrow night
when the show returns to find life out.
For another day of America's tuned-in radioed troubles
to yet again start over.

      ✳

2. *The Intern*

Because it's radio and their voices are smooth, because it's sex

they air, the hosts get more fan mail than their looks deserve.
Dr. Judy, one man demurs, must be a vixen. But I know best,
having worked the late shift at the station. "Subbing,"
they call it, when the normal host goes face down
in the free tequila handed out at Promotions.
I'm the one left standing who sets the Demods
up for Go, passes Tylenol and headphones out
like Kleenex in the control room. When the call for me first
came through it wasn't unusual:

for female DJ's, radio's a magnet for solitudes
who think the visual is an imposition.
By midnight, we're anyone's face.

                    "Do you pull your panties off one leg
at a time?" he'd asked. "Do you like to suck your fingers?"
"Screw you," I said and hung up. But the threat must have come off
as an imperative; every night at twelve o'clock, he calls.
"I can tell you're smart," he said after our third conversation.
"You don't want to suck my cock, do you?"

                    Meanwhile Judy's regulars complain
about the soullessness of dating. "It's like,"
says caller number two, "I have this deep dark hole
I just can't fill." Which is, Jagger proclaims, just
what we're here to do. Night's for the Lonely Hearts: jokers

scratching bathroom stalls full
of phone numbers who find our hotline call-in stapled
next to posters of Asian girls and Danish cheerleaders
broadcasting universal *help help help*

translated to *show* and *more show.* So
"Let's talk more about her deep, dark hole,"
Jagger growls, and I picture stars sucked like cue balls
into crushing space pockets centimeters wide; perhaps (this
with guilt) a thirteen-year-old and her first makeshift
shortwave radio in a blacked-out park,
letting the world's silky tongues roll over her.

For better or for worse, settling on us. And always: Let's talk
more about this hole, this cavity of yours eaten out
by increasing addictions to toll-free numbers; trash's sweet,
singular anxieties—

       "I'll bet you're married," The Pervert said last night.
Tricked into intimacy, I'd forgotten myself and answered, "No."
"I knew it," he replied. "You just don't sound
like you'd listen to that kind of garbage."

I'm starting to think of it like advice.

        ✴

3. Dr. Judy

Famous lie: "I got into radio
because it's not т.v." When such desolate
wave lengths measure up basically the same.
Space fascinates us.
Where we find it we tend to add

and add what we cannot see, as when
the atom is revealed to be a truck-sized sack
with a few peanuts rolling in it
and we counter with cushions of charge

stuffed within, nearly undetectable by microscope or laser,
because the truth that, at points, the hand
is indistinguishable from the table due to
nothing terrifies. It's *nothing*

that connects us here in space just as *nothing*
is the key to Caitlin's lover's changed desire,
the space in and out between them, electric

hips pushed against each other
by the kitchen sink. What is still
uncharted land, the soul?
we've asked. No, space.
And sent men into it, monkeys; even

a woman or two has arrived back from that crushing
blue-black with bowls
of sterile dirt, the frozen crust hurled off stars
eons ago. We're amazing

ourselves more than this eternal flotsam can,
which is the soul of space

we tell ourselves, the greatest moral that exists
recast in paperweights,
health drinks, easy-to-get-in shoes.
Tang and Velcro are what we've communally gained
from the moon, I've often said.
We're a culture that values
T-shirts, pelts, evidence

of the exotic. "Any response means hope tonight,"
I tell my audience. "Take scalps,

lovers. What's wrong?" *Oh*
nothing nothing nothing! But all the peanuts
rattling in their sacks tell me: It's space
between us and the world, hands
dangling through chairs and vice-versa,
the uncertainty of blood pushed mightily
through the yam-sized heart and all we've got
to show for discontent

are postcards: the husband's
nightie. The scarf of leather studs
your mother wears to our reunion. And worse:
this man who takes my daughter in the bathroom
like a drug when I'm not home.

"Just talk to me," says our intern tonight to the hot-
line phone while somewhere over Minsk
a satellite broadcasts every language on the Earth,
including whale songs, weakly.
Our safety catch in terse hellos.

Our greeting to the universe.

the structure of pluto

Whose only moon is Charon, ferryman of the dead
who circles death's king.
No cartoon dog this, Pluto brings its own
rules to the table: sheets

of rock and frozen methane, an icy mantle of ammonia
that cloaks in a perfume like cleansing fluid.
If there are dead vacationing in the eternal,
they might be torn here between attractions
of oblivion and remembrance.

Charon is half the size of its parent planet.

Death and its fan club thus revolve through weight
and gravitation almost
balanced: the one threatening to pull the other
into its frozen orbit.

Cold is the language

Hell spoke in through Dante, yes, Auden noted it was chilly
the day Yeats died and it was winter the night
I read illicit excerpts of Yeats's
unpublished notebook, copied
by my lover under the ammonial green light of a law firm's Xerox.
We crouched before my apartment's picture
window revealing the world

Disneyfied by static, snow under which my lover's car
froze and our will to separate got buried
inch by inch. He worked on copyrights:
this was his first case. For this
he'd simply heard YEATS, slipped

what he could from its maroon folder,
its dead syllables
leashed to the notebook's lines
as if by gravity. *Someone has to care, if not me,*
he'd thought; perhaps *Someone has to care about me,*
which phrases twined into one orbit, weighted
equally with their own cold
persuasions.

This is what my boyfriend thought: to drag
his love-gift in over a thousand protestations.
He would have done anything to impress

upon me what tied, the structure
of our sex intricate and unvaried as if fatal, as if
kisses were isotopes that radiated.
Or we were planetary: our shared affection no more faithful
than a hood of methane.

There was nothing in those notebooks

that needed protection. Nothing private
of the great poet ferried from the Otherworld.
All we learned was that he had terrible handwriting. *But*
why shouldn't I love most the accomplished?
This I learned, as months later I learned to say *Hell*

would be staying with you forever
to this man who brought me entry,
language like an irradium of hail, white-hot
silicate raining through space forever.
I learned to be cruel as protection, poling
between this
desire and that, love's boredom stiffened in each cell.

This is not the only galaxy in the universe.
This is not the only planet, the coldest one, even further
from our star than Neptune, which itself is plagued by windstorms.
Years before a lawyer brought me poems from the dead.

Faithful dog, what keeps you here?

the planets whisper. And watch each night, attracted
to the brilliance of men we still believe

are found in stars.

When nature wins it's with small things,
usually signalled by a compromise:
anemones attached to crabs for food,
ciliated cells meshed to the phagocytic.
Familiarity shows the how and where to
hurt. It's the intimacy that does us in.

II

rogue's gallery

The ear is important. Within its nautilus
blend of shell and skin, its delicate, pink

configurations, lies a world of ridges;
difference almost as useful as a fingerprint

or kiss. As with snowflakes, no two
aural profiles are the same, facts

that the French appreciated
first in convicts and that I've come

to blame for my attraction
to mug shots, the sterile

photos where everyone
looks away.

All my lovers face a wall
in pictures I snap, trained to fake

that pose exposing the bitter drum,
the silky lobe's slubs and lace, nipped in—

each one individual in size
and taste. I don't pretend to love

you, but the ear is important.
Any side street or grocery is a precinct

with its threats,
its blotters and staring.

And I always approach the world
sideways, I've told you, when your great seal-

like torso hints to loom
over this salt body, when even

breathing makes air feel
drawn up, tight, small, sudden

as a noose. I spend my single days
by open windows and photographs

of mountain profiles, raccoons hedging
in the shocking light of a car beam.

Nobody, I've told the speaker's black mesh
whorls, loves freedom

more than I do. And watched gulls explode
up from the walk like gray prisoners storming

the Bastille, the world in mirrors
carefully placed so that only the corners

of an eye must identify things. Me, in the half-
light, shy, unsmiling. And you watching me.

Head-on. Still trying.

bodice ripper: romance with subtext

Handsome Dante Fowler had known many women,
which bothers him now even introduction's interest
has waned. Sex. The eternal coin toss. And
though none had captured his heart the way Angel had,
daily he finds this auburn histrionic display of "virgin
sacrifice" less intriguing; the staged rapes,
squabbles about some Daytona lace heiress, a ploy
he'll call "Flame" fizzled out. Love?
A tennis ball being squeezed through his windpipe.
ECSTASY'S SLOW EMBRACE. Thus, page 306,
Charmaine Lamoureux, who *never dreamed*
the tall, handsome stranger would steal her innocence,
we could read as the smarter one.
When Rand McAllister gambles his ex out of home
in Texas, on the way drunkenly buying Charmaine
at the whorehouse she didn't know wasn't *a motel,*
"Well, at least I'm not bored," she can argue,
fate having maintained enough cheap thrills this once
to keep the cerebrum's sex drive interested.

Consumed by his kisses, each night she'd long for DEFIANT
RAPTURE, plods the plot that Desire, our abstract,
astonishes with violence. LOVE ME WITH FURY,
GOLDEN TORMENT, SWEET SAVAGE HEART,
could be the chalky inscriptions tattooed on Sweet
Tarts passed in fistfuls 'round any classroom.
Or a prelude to spike that serialized dullness:
"Eternal love? You mean, like, marriage?" just where the spineless
paperback stops. *Each day voluptuous Charmaine*
questions her decision to remain in her husband's world—

There are arguments. Since a cousin deposited herself
and her broken teeth like a set of dishes on their doorstep,
Charmaine's suspected the junkie fiction they have dwindled to.
"I can't live without" the script goes before bathtubs
and hallway closets across America. *Though by night,*
when Rand crushes her in his masculine arms—
They drink their drinks. They watch the stars.
Two ships passing, etc. "It's not," the novelist says, "exactly science
that we're writing here."

Today Dante's caught

his Angel in a calculated swoon. A photo-op: one hand scoops
her skull arch while the other travels south, crushing limp
buttocks. "More sensual!" the cover painter cries. He etches sun
in Dante's fading hair, points to his prop
of cardboard, champagne-spackled cloud. DESIRE'S EBB?
LUSTFUL FLUX? More pink in everyone's cheeks.
Such are, the painter knows, the rules for painting schlock:
some glow at least should be portrayed. If we call it beautiful,
he knows we'll call it good. He knows
we'd like to believe words
alter only the parts of us we want them to.

crescent down works factory

The smell inside the workroom is warm and fecal,
birdlike from the goose down in nylon bags.
My hand grips the nozzle of the vacuum.
The digital scale ticks off weight measurements like time
on a surreal clock. It's sensitive enough to take my pulse,
weigh out blood. I pry each coat shell open
delicately, like a surgeon peeling skin from a patient's skull
so as not to rip the Gortex and render the product
unusable. Strap the down bag on the vacuum,
adjust the nozzle to the hole. Blow in down
until each seamed tubing in the jacket resembles papier-
mâché: round and slick to the fingers, so light
it feels hollow. I swallow aspirin, slide the tuning dial
on the radio. I can feel myself getting feverish.
At nine-thirty break today, I thought the bags
had saints' hands. The digits seized and twitched
like epileptics on the screen. To sleep I crouched
by the seamstresses. They woke me, quarter to ten,
with orders and to tell me, in broken English,
down destroys lungs. Never work without your mask.
Months ago I ran my hands through it
carelessly, entranced: the silky motes
like apple blossoms, like clouds of pollen or
spider sacks. Now I know it travels through the mouth
in bacterial chains, weakens lungs, infects blood.
I imagine each red platelet turning white so that,
instead of running when I am cut, my blood will fly
away. After work now I pick each soft bud

from shirt and hair, shower immediately to rinse away
work's stink. Even through the mask
I can smell it. I take more aspirin. It tastes like down.

At night in the tub my pubic hair seems dusted with it.
It looks like snow, you said, combing it
with a finger. After six months
we've both grown tired of the comparison. Tired even
of the body that looks the same in each unveiling,
though you groaned the first time you saw it.
Tonight I'll slip the rubber on your cock's tip, roll it down
slow. Swing a leg over your still, prone torso
and mount in just the way we're used to, my face
leaning into yours. Is that good? Oh yes, oh yes,
your body shaking, hands twisted
into the white sheet. I'll kiss you
and we'll both taste it. My breath like a bird, lungs
aching with the strain of holding back the wings'
wild thrash. Your body could kill me, I think.
And the snow outside falls quietly around us, like stars.

the night my mother meets bruce lee

China smokes under a tree. That's how low
        mist settles in this picture, bad brush painting
where silver maids crouch like silver wolves
        wailing for a man who'll come
from the moon. There are dishes. In the restaurant
        my mother loads up red tubs
of spilled noodles, shuffles toward the one white
        customer who watches. *You know the story
behind that painting?* My mother doesn't.
        The man's face falls, a little florid, too
open like the jar of her mother's pastel
        peonies so enormous with want, she can't
believe these are flowers her own mother
        displays on waxed tabletops, petals arranged
in shredded pleats as if the flower were swelling
        in its own desire. She doesn't know anything,
my mother: not the fat and dirty carp in its tank,
        what the inscrutable phoenix rises out of.
Autumn leaves are falling like rain is a poem which never
        penetrates the bell-shaped, woolen skirt hand-
sewn thankfully *sans* poodle, *sans* glitter peony,
        rough as her nails, which glisten only
when varnished with the grease of someone else's leftovers.
        All my neighbors are barbarians and you,
you are a thousand miles away is a tune
        from a distinctly different planet
where radio towers do not thrum with
        Buddy Holly, mothers never chide in strange
tongues. My mother has a smile trained
        to kindle nebula, hurl satellites into space.

No, she doesn't have the willowy thighs of any
        of the seven maids hanging in their one frame,
the bangs of a Veronica Lake.
        Now the newest busboy erupts
out of the back kitchen, Vesuvian, a smatter
        of duck fat and ash.
"I come from Hong Kong from real
        Chinese," he told my mother. Posed
with martial vigilance, scared the cook,
        cut his thumb on a knife blade. *Kung*
Fooey everyone at the restaurant
        calls him who wields his shoulders like pickaxes
and leers at the waitresses. *I hate that*
        son of a bitch, mumbles the cashier.
The busboy mugs: a film star by the fire escape.
        What I wouldn't do to be famous, my mother thinks.
The answer's nothing. My mother will do
        nothing to be famous. *Although my neighbors*
are barbarians and you, you are a thousand
        miles away, there are always
two cups at my table a song
        on the restaurant tape drones mysteriously.
Customers file past my mother, a prop
        in the dullest film of all time. She'll buy
a cashmere sweater in pink tonight,
        take herself to the pictures on Sunday. At sixteen,
my mother thinks it's what
        she's supposed to want. She thinks
it's going to make her happy.

you're sick, jesse . . . sick, sick, sick

says a cow to
the cow grilling steak in
     Larson's field.
Meat-smoke ladders
white sky between them as
     Jesse,

one dismayed car-
toon hoof nudging the black
     spatula,
continues to
grill. The other cows stare.
     How to

chastise the cow
that eats cow; the coral
     snake attached
to its tail by
familiar depressions
     of its

own clear teeth? What
should Jesse love most but
     Jesse him-
self? Differences
undo each other, strength
     cancel-

ling strength, like the
drab forest bird whose
        faster, red
hybrid chick can't
mesh with its environ-
        ment for

color. Sex, like
dinner, has serious
        consequences.
Better, Jesse
thinks, to indulge himself,
        auto-

erotic:
he's a real self-starter.
        Jesse's steak
smokes. The cows stare.
It's a cartoon spelling
        God's law

against Jesse.
But whose private sympa-
        thies don't err
sometimes toward Tar-
zan's luckless cannibals
        licking

their chops over
the vacant cauldron; to
      Onan a-
postate not an
apostle? Whose *Being* being
      never

morbid, cartoon-
ish, self-
      devouring?

captain cook in tahiti discovers tattooing: an event that has subtle but important consequences for my parents and myself

July 1769. King George Island. His first adventure
in diplomacy and all Cook can think about is food.
"I am of opinion that Victuals dress'd this way
are more juicy than by any of our methods, large fish
in particular, Bread fruit, Bananoes and Plantains Cook'd
like boild Potatoes—" Food and tattoos. It's dusk.
In a glow of candlenuts men sweat sullenly
over pineapple while the women rush off to stuff themselves
in private. That's when Cook notices: those *Z*s
toothed to knuckle and toe, crescents so blackly apparent, "so various
that both their quantity and situation seem to depend
entirely on the Humour of the individual." The Captain winces,
struggles to put more breadfruit away. Next morning
his first journalistic record is the cheiftain's arched buttocks,
tiari's black curlicues smoking up each thigh as the man
drags in his breakfast.

*

"I'd work skin any day," says this month's "Slinging Ink" feature.
Skin Rag has blown up the tats so big a veil of sweat
gleams through like priming. "Though I admit
the gun buzz bothers me." On Saturdays my father
shaved behind closed doors. If I asked I could watch the flat
blade sucking over throat skin, then sit on our clean black couch
while mother vacuumed our stairwell. She hates the sound
of blades. "The Colour they use is lamp black
prepared from the smook of a kind of oily nutt," wrote Cook.
"The Instrument bone or shell struck into the skin so deep
every stroke is followed with a small quantity of blood."
Smokey Vaselines my thigh, watches skin
shrivel pink under his gun. Blood's pucker. A steady,
cupped rasp of bees. To take my mind off the pain I think
of anything: doughnuts, a wedding album. My father's face
and hair so pale beside his darker bride. I remember
for their anniversary I hung red *Fook* signs between doorways,
watched cellophane and ticker curl arterially
till the hours he drove home wakened deep moonrises,
set the night ink bleeding like an octopus over the city.

Why get one? Cook wondered, though the question wasn't really
why but *when.* "As this is a painfull operation," he noted,
"it is perform'd but once in their life time, never
until they are 12 or 14 years of age." Once is fine with me.
But "If I had bare white skin again," says Smokey's girl, Carleen,
"I'd start getting those tattoos." My mother won't
give blood, get shots or share combs, calls ear piercing
barbaric. A cultural tick, she argues. The mark
of the lower class. After a lunch of plantains Cook limps
beachward to watch sailors cavort with local girls, whose lower
faces, ink-starred, collapse in muddy smiles. Cook knows
what lives abroad can't work at home. He gives them time.
And there's sympathy for them, as when he notes the sailors'
longings muffled behind bathhouses and canoes; the men and women
who "look upon it as a freedom from which they value themselves"
wrestling into each other. Proteans evolving second forms.
After a month he sees even his starchiest officers work nude.
And on their bare backs: black arches. Flat, elliptical moons.

*

I figure I can hide it; just never change clothes when she's around.
"This'll Last Longer Than Your Marriage!" *Tat-Way*'s slogan boasts
beside its graphic: a knife plunged into a bleeding cupcake.
Paris, 1968. Mother sends her telegram announcing the wedding
two days after New Year's. "I'm sorry," it says.
"But I wanted to." No, from my experience nothing is as foreign
to her as apology. And by this time the Kans must have expected it;
not one child of theirs yet married Chinese. But white?
No gifts shuttle via mail, no congratulations are exchanged.
Most don't know to what depth artists repeatedly place the pigment,
nor where it rests—whether in corium, melanin layer, bottom
of the dermis, the papillae. Fact is, the tattoo's permanence
is due to the thin cyst layered beneath pigment, the failing of skin
to eject the unknown elements. "There is no denying the high
sexual significance of tattoing," writes Phil Andros.
Which might explain my mother's furtive examination
of my dresser drawers when she discovers the cache of tattoo magazines,
the way she tries surprising me in the shower when visiting
by lurking behind the bathroom door.

*

"This just expresses the crazy side of me," says Carleen,
flexing her abs. "Since we're both smokers, a Zippo
seemed appropriate." Smokey's thin blade digs shamelessly
toward my pelvis and I speculate on my parents' possible reactions;
recall Stainsby writing behind Cook's back: "Myself,
and some others of our company, underwent the operation
and had our arms marked." No one knows what happened to him.
He might have been beheaded in the later raid. Or he made it
back to England by chance, where his reluctant wife
(his mistress? the young male lover, perhaps?) recoiled at sight
of flesh pebbled blackly. But then she too became accustomed
enough that the sight of his lined chest made palms sweat
with longing. Like lying in the arms of savages, being devoured
by geometry— Which might have been the way
my mother expressed her new husband's body to herself, their uncharted
skins marbled by the weak Paris street lights coming off the sill.
"We're never coming back," she writes. Though they do,
hand-in-hand, resigned to three months' pregnancy.
"One little tat," says Carleen. "That's all it took for me."

*

"—fathom water an owsey bottom, the shore of bay a sandy beach—"
Imagine the sight of new land, islands like stockings in a tub of water.
My father and mother step down from their respective
trains and scan La Gare Nord in its grainy fog, the smell of dogs
and coffee wafting toward them from the Metro. Vendors
yawn their customers aside; two Algerians hurry into a cafe.
"They are of various colours, nay some of the women
are almost as fair as Europeans," mused Cook
upon first meeting the Tahitians. Which thought occurred
to my father, perhaps, seeing my mother six years after school's passage
and a stint in the air force. The autumn, like her hair,
smelled of rain. "With tattoos you never have to go cruising
the bars or baths, looking for beauty."—*Skin Rag*
No indeed, it stays with you. Sun springs hotly
from its cloud and the stationary trains wait like capped needles.
Smokey, done, hands me cellophane. My parents-to-be
(sensing this? sensing me?) stop in their tracks, blinded
by this sight of each other. Round the bed of bay Cook's men
spy the beach, the chieftain and his tattooed daughters waiting.
Slowly his sailors lower their oars.
Then cover their eyes in greeting.

Scientists, to find what makes someone attractive, generated composites of heads through graphics, superimposing them to create new ones. Faces composed of the most graphics were judged to be most beautiful, being round as fullerenes, smog-skinned, symmetrical and anonymous as soccer balls.

III

on getting a dog and being told that
what i really want is a child

For years I considered the journey. What meals
I'd make, what cities I'd conquer, the foreign thighs

of walls tattooed with graffiti. I imagined
the exhaustion of mornings up,

without a home, the pushing on, and thought
of sailors hovering the frozen

river crusts, or the way stones
struck the mouth of Magellan walking

through the Verzin gates. How they burst
through lip and gums! And how dangerous

their animals must have seemed to him with their yellow
faces and small teeth. And then, of course, I thought

about how Magellan knew his men all hated him, the one
Portugese on a ship of Spaniards, irritating and obvious

as a nipple. How they plotted
to revolt at each intersection of the sea

and cheered when the unknown natives
threw stones. Perhaps I am promiscuous,

the way some sailors choose to love
themselves on long journeys

and Magellan, when he reached each new port,
lay on its fish-rotted quay

and sobbed. What I want
is the dust of towns, canyons

full of dead seas and the sun a killing god. No need
for wars or discipline,

to make my body a bark
for others cast adrift, bobbing like buoys

or ice flows. *There are monsters on the Pole,* Magellan wrote.
And giants, a handsome people.

Though he never knew what to say of the woman
who crawled aboard his boat to see if it was true:

that dinghies suckle from the mother ship like pups
from wooden bitches. And snuck a loosened nail deep

inside herself to carry as she hobbled home,
nursing it in secret

as if its iron
was really gold.

night sweeper

Everywhere I think of young women with unwashed
      faces, men
asleep against their stomachs. I miss morning's semen
      smell. And time
before first light when you emerged tucked
      into mufflers
and suits like cages to sweep the driveway for exercise,
      the clock
of your ticking broom timing sleeplessness shared in twos.
      Now
for hours I toss awake massaging the muscles of my eyes
      with a finger.
Beside me lies an unshuffled Lucky pack
      and poker chips.
There are cards I draw which tell the future.

      *

Last summer I wanted to lay down: another body. Become
      the skunk's broom
tail, up, huffing it out past the driveway. Each night
      you were clean
without purpose or timeliness. You did not make love
      like the angry
couple next door nor forage like the skunk for food scraps
      to be excavated
under the moon. The car park's photo eye bled you
      into dark.
An early wind conspired to consume the soft furnace
      of the yard's fire

even as you stood counting and counting rows of leaves.
    Twelve piles now:
one for each couplet of my life. Still, you appeared torn
    between them
as if every decision carried equal weight, every problem its own
    terrific sorrow.
Assuming this as well, I'd like to analyze my hair
    for a moment.
Shanks of it unpinned, lifted at random, display streaks
    of white
like Christmas lights threading a black barroom. I think it has
    something to do with lack
of sleep. I think it has something to do with your broom.
    Its metronomic
sweep timing dawn, hiss hiss hissing every night away according
    to your particular schedule.
I should tell you how every year I plan to step down
    and be reborn,
sloe-eyed Aphrodite, in the gin-baths and blackjack of the damned.
    I'm moving
to the desert to become as greedy as the sun; I will fasten there
    until by time
alone I am endemic: manure to earth, plague
    to Europe.
I don't need good examples or clean driveways. I need sleep.
    Hours
to whittle into nothing more than plastic cups of beer
    or dust balls,
movies too awful to pay for. I want to waste
    a life away
being homesick. I thought this having smelled
    the unwashed

crease of your neck, your wretched shoulder elongated
        as an ox's haunch.
People are tender with me because they think I can't bear the weight
        of insomnia, and thus
mistake my blank expressions for anger. That was my blank face
        at the window
watching you, sir, watching you sweep what looked to be enormous
        white cups
from the walk. I was disappointed with the repetition
        of sleeplessness,
for though my hair is turning white I've had nothing to worry over,
        not a child
or lover, not one word so beautiful as to make sleep
        an impossibility.

        ✳

Somewhere there is a store filled with bone artifacts
        which I will enter
late at night to parcel out each rib among the shelves, lock my thighs
        behind the counter.
And I will dream there in my separate houses of skunks chased
        by errant brooms,
grass tips dark as a girl's boots. Even the girl, my metaphor, will
        rise naked
from her bath of cards brushing stones from her chest. This
        is how I learned
you died today: at noon, having found the new postwoman
        asking for you.
At your door was a sign I'd ignored since Monday,
        underneath
the penciled scrawls of several residents. He's dead,
        I exclaimed,

and she covered her little wax mouth with a hand, comical,
    ashamed.
But it means nothing to us. I knew your smell, the sound
    of your broom.
I began to write about them months ago simply as an exercise
    to help me sleep.
Now I'm simply getting the chance to finish up; now, sometimes,
    I sleep.
Tonight I might dye my hair in anticipation of events which decades
    won't provide,
note the papers taking over the drive, the stones and late autumn
    cherry pits,
unswept, bunched in fists. I'm waiting to be a wife. I have my cards,
    my lights,
my thousand useless bottles. Insomnia was only a tiny space
    between us.
This was your life to me; it was nothing at the time.
    And this
is my acknowledgment. This is just an exercise.

drink me

read my mother's medicine vials, comically
stated on her dresser like blue exclamations, a row
of lovely threats. And so I drank
two teaspoons an hour for fever while growing
so small myself—all my sixteen years of ribs—
I could vanish between gray sheets, a ceiling and a bed.

That was the year the Challenger burst
from the gate bearing you, its school teacher.
This was news I was too tired to change. I lay
chewing my teaspoon, watching the sky
inhale your shuttle like a crumb off a plate.
Four hundred years ago to the day Sir Francis Drake
drowned off the coast of Panama. This I learned
at school along with notes on hurricanes, typhoons,
oceanic whirlpools that, like a house's drain,
sink clockwise according to their position near the equator.
A drain, a crumb, a plate: the world described
in such familiar terms *even a girl,* my teacher said,
could fathom it. Florida's white sky gleamed
in its cage and the world, for you, became
particled as an ashtray's contents flung mid-air.
I remember the end of Houston's warning "technical,"
the crowd at the thin wire compound.
In the backdrop: white smoke on white sky,
a row of pale flags nodding at the ground.

*

Had you ever asked life to slip you from the anonymous, unsure
of the space a wall provides? Centuries ago
men sailed boats loaded with breadfruit and Maori girls
startling only for their *mokos* while every night
for me there was your fragile body knocking
against God like a clapper in its bell, the fat moon
slowly losing its charm. A decade before I thought
I might go up in space. I was wrong.
A seashell, a sleeve of dust might content me now.

That was the year my bed became a black hole
from which I escaped through the silent warren
of clothes drawers, the highballs and tumblers
snuck by the dish rack. I slept on the library's
roof in summer, burrowed against ravine sides
for my enormous freedom.
Every night was lovely, Christa. The yellow stars
and lights, those first ripe sips of beer. For a while
it was like I had discovered something. Almost
like I was going somewhere.

joe louis and the war effort, or how my grandfather acquired the laundromat

1. We had so many more stories then
        a taxi wasn't enough to hold them all
and my grandfather had to win a laundromat on a dollar.
        That was the year a U.S. naval base exploded
to dockbits, saltpeter, and lampshades
        got made from human skin. George, my Chinese
grandfather, didn't bet on this. March 27th, 1942:
        at 6 P.M. he and Y, the Japanese neighbor,
sit under spools of lamplight in a wet basement playing cards,
        silently wagering the future. Ten years before,
my grandmother wore a placard round her neck that read, "I am Chinese,"
        to distinguish herself. But George, now, is willing
to put aside differences for a friend, he says, taking Y
        into his confidence. *Draw a card.* He knows within days
Y will be on a train bound for camp in Idaho.
        You'll give it back? Y asks. *When I return?* George nods.
Y's deed for the laundry slips atop their pile of quarters.
        And in my grandfather's hand: pocket lint, a knife-length scar,
a house that's full of hearts.

        *

2. Even in Chinatown Joe Louis is beautiful.

They've got photos of him tacked beside Miss June, a knot
of red papers like exposed nerve endings sparkling between them.

The Wah Mee Gambling Club gathers its disaffected regulars
to take the pulse of racetracks, scores of baseball teams

nightly scrawled on paper scraps, pored over like the mysteries
of I Ching. George's hands have eczema sores the size

of horrible roses his children like to paint with gum
before he rides off in his taxi. And in the future, May 1970:

at four o'clock Joe Louis will owe over a million dollars
to the government and be deemed insane. But this Friday

it's nine o'clock, March 27th at the Garden, where Simon
is getting the worst of it. They've unpenned the enlisted Louis

from Upton and a sea of khaki greets him ringside. Every fan's
soldiering today: they've all got crew cuts, weight pills,

a fascination for sparring. Meanwhile on grandfather's street,
Y sits alone tuned to the match on KCTZ imagining country

brown and flat as an eternal boxing ring. He ticks off
destinations like so many famous names: Camp Harmony, Minidoka,

Dempsey, Willard, Schmeling, Poston, Baer, Shufflin' Joe—
The Brown Bomber, Manzanar. A seamless stream

of faces on cards, weight and shoe size listed
next to occupation. Beside him (he dreams) Willard on the red sofa

lectures Baer on the ending possibilities of white men
in the ring, his crooked right paw ticking off

Louis's supposed faults. *We can't lose,* Louis bumbles tonight
about the war. *'Cause we're on God's side.* The crowd

howls, showers popcorn on the path before him
while inside the Wah Mee men trade green fistfuls under his black

and white photo image that flickers by with every breeze,
that passes silently right through them.

*

3. What's at stake is what we know is already lost.

When my grandfather smiled, counted out his cards,
for a moment Y feared his life—not the laundry, livelihood of sons—
he'd sold. He trusts George more than he trusts anyone
on the block, which isn't saying much.

They've never been friends. What's to bet later
he returns to find the laundry sold, the Kans disappeared?

Imagine history then. Outside of Eden evacuees
hang wet clothes to dry on wire. Schmeling staggers
in the ring while in Shanghai a bayoneted
woman feels what might be the hot
black tip of her cervix peeking from her gown.
It is the decade my grandmother refuses to speak to the Japanese
and every day more families disappear as if in love
with the ice trucks and pigeon sellers'
meandering rounds, called by Change: their piper.
I'm working in hell, says the gas station attendant
on Cherry Street. This was part of Seattle's Chinatown where Y
and my grandfather lived. I live here, too, four blocks away.
You should move, my grandmother says. *It's dangerous now.*
I agree but still do nothing. Each day I pass the block that housed
the laundromat, Wimpey's, the Bailey Gatzer School
where garbage lay in strangling sheets degrading into grass;
where Wonder Bread, the west coast factory, now triumphs.
Our street was cordoned off because of sniper fire once.

The quiet off the street, when it came, haunted our empty house.
After awhile only the hum of distant sirens could settle it; the gentle
pop pop pops, like breathing on a microphone,
help us get to sleep.

*

4. *Progress,* the gamblers at the Wah Mee say about the war,
     is taking advantage of a situation.
George nods, ear trained to KCTZ. By the eighth so much rests
     on Simon's fall even God would bet against him.
Most likely, the bouncer says, *he won't come back.*
     You know, on account of them they've started to kill Chinese.
He can't imagine that in 1983 five Vietnamese
     will slip along the Wah Mee's silver corridor with rifles,
killing everyone except my grandfather
     who's at the laundry with Y's son and dies instead
from cancer. *They were rivals,* they would claim in court.
     It was a war. But now suddenly a drink lies heavier in the mouth
and *That's not why I did it,* says George, who's speaking now
     of time. *It's time,* he begins, but never finishes, his audience
having slipped away to the reality of the match.
     And I wish he'd meant to say: *To put aside history*
pertinent to old customs—a country fewer
     and fewer of us recognize. This is what I want him to mean.
In just two days the laundry will be his, though he'll always refuse
     its possession, this trust he's safekeeping. I know: he gives it back.
But no one listens to him. *Louis is one Hok Wee,* someone says,⁻
     fingering his drink. *I hear he even dates a white girl.*
At this, three gamblers in their booth laugh. Women,
     they know, can be such whores. Tired, broke, slightly bored,
my grandfather slips out of his seat under the lamp's good eye
     to outside, where the moon flickers gold like a
buckle unsnapping. It's Seattle. It's 1942. Tonight, even in Chinatown
     Joe Louis is beautiful. And no one thinks twice about betting.

other people's success

One of the most famous Brazilian poets, Manuel Bandeira, was presented with a
permanent parking space in front of his apartment house . . . with an enameled
sign POETA—although he never owned a car and didn't know how to drive.
—ELIZABETH BISHOP

This is what you've been waiting for: parking spaces
    littered across town with your name on them, useless

shower of bus tokens in mailbags that clog your doorway.
    So many other people wander under the enviable

cloud of paeans you've always wanted, now you have arrived to find them
    in full throaty blossom: free tickets, magazine interviews,

companionship with the other stellar literary immovables
    over coffee or C-SPAN discussion groups about the state

of unified discography or philately or maybe even
    poetry. People will ask your advice now about the most esoteric

subjects just to hear you speak. Listen! That voice! They know
    this is the same epiglottis and windpipe that have composed

your lush stanzas, those lyrical nodes complete
    strangers have been known to weep over, such as "Love hurts," or

"My friend, they've already sold the doughnuts / And we, we are the last
    of the true restaurateurs." Even if the poem in its entirety

has been degraded in the public's imagination to no more
    than, "Sing, goddess," followed by your inevitable, "The end,"

this is enough for them to love you. This is enough
    for the adoring glances everywhere of undergraduates

at black-tie affairs with the rich food that is sending you,
    rapidly, to pot. You are ballooning with your own triumphs!

The senate will create an entirely new position for you
    and a younger generation waste years mimicking

your particular blend of abstract realism and *joie de vivre*
    that annoys no one. Poeta! Even now

you are eating a bowl of creamed asparagus soup in a darkened
    restaurant in which the waiter arrives at opportune intervals

to whisper, *Brava!* in your ear. Even if you spill soup on your blouse,
    your lap, your velvet shoes, you know the patrons will still beg

More! Say something, sing your beautiful songs! Just as a girl
    might stare at your lovely ruined costume while her mother

wipes away an eyelash stuck like a black tear to her cheek. It flutters
    under their excited breaths. *Make a wish and blow,*

the mother says, and the girl looks at you wordlessly, inhaling.
    Recite us something, poet! the restaurant clamors. Now you open

your mouth as if to speak and the girl instead flies out.
    At last! she cries, in perfect meter. Your final poem.

Do you not see that nature is clamouring for two things only, a body free from pain, a mind released from worry and fear for the enjoyment of pleasurable sensations?

—Lucretius, *The Nature of the Universe*

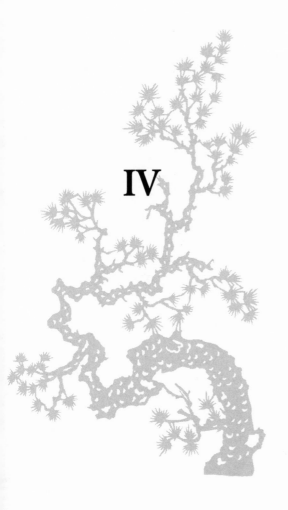

IV

convocation

1. Why Torture?

Pain is a threshold that changes. Thus muses Bacon, 1597,
at the torture of John Gerard. This Jesuit priest they racked
and beat three years off and on, after the report he "did receive
a packet of letters out of the Low Countries . . . he being
noted to be a great intelligencer and to hold correspondence
with traitors beyond the seas." Bacon leans against the Tower
wall chewing his thumb. "To resolve nature," he's thinking,
"into abstraction is less to our purpose than to dissect her
into parts." Perhaps Bacon thinks
less of himself cranking the strappado, buckling
down the screws. Perhaps he appreciates the weight
of torture's doing. But Gerard's no saint
or even falsely accused prophet.
He's no simple William Hacket mounted on a cart
in Cheapside convinced he's Christ. Whose arms they tied
to drafts in the market, yanked out like stubborn teeth.
Though Bacon may feel sympathy, this isn't the anonymous
father accused falsely of sedition who broke himself
for family's sake under the weights, knowing that to confess
meant the property of his children would be seized
by the state. *Peine forte et dure.* We don't like to think
what pressing would entail: the weights, at first enough
to be sustained, increased gradually till one's internal organs
burst. It can last nine days if you are given water.
In torture manuals the body's tender points are elaborately
labelled L and D, *latus, dorsus,* the head under its curve of C
drawn aghast with horror. It's amazing that they draw the pain.
So Bacon's unconcern might pale compared with fact, this man

pressed, nude and grey with stone dust, the victim
of a choice. Though injustice comes to mind it's really *sacrifice*
illuminating purpose here: a parent willing flesh
as flesh reaped, sown; that time's intangible path should thread
through houses, a cast about the eyes or mouth so like
and yet so distant. This is loyalty. It is said even Hacket
had a child or two, though he left them nothing.
Because of poverty, he had no choice but torture. He died instead
a pauper's death, on record calling all saints as witnesses
to gather. To come for the insane, the broken and dog-eared.
To come for him, a poor man like Christ: simply a body for the heirs.

*

2. Why Not?

The child claims to hate her. After the two hour drive, no
ice cream at the supermarket. Haven't we all
eschewed a parent once in pique? This evening
my friend is close to tears, her five-year-old denying interest
in speaking to her on the phone. "He's eating dinner,"
her ex says, trying for supplication. Across the line she hears
television's comic blare, the stepmother worrying
a new toy before him on the carpet. But though, she says,
she can rationalize her child's behavior lacking
logic for her own, this isn't enough to stop
unrecognition's pain; the disinterest shown
when she shouts his name above the din of other whispers,
the cars and slot-machine gumballs of every
attractive passerby. Perhaps to her what is of interest
about Bacon's torturing at the trial is not how he endured
the sight of men eviscerated, but that he went on
as a scientist who recommended repeated and controlled
experiments. *The New Atlantis.* After torture
what is pain? "It is not," Bacon wrote, "the lie
that passeth through the mind, but the lie that sinketh in,
and settleth in it, that doth the hurt." My friend assumes
that torture stopped because human life
became more valuable, though it was for proof
that we redefined the laws. Coercive force (surprise)
might make one lie under pressure.
So "I hate you," children everywhere say as once, in anger,
I stuck crayoned "For Sale" signs above my father's bed.
"He won't admit it," my mother says, "but it really hurt him."
It's a lie families depend upon to work: father's gloss

of patience, gentle understanding from mother. We played it like a card trick all the years I was growing up. This sacrifice of one *(so easy! so natural!)* for anger's privilege in the other.

*

3. And How to Do It?

Particle *and* wave. Light that spackles and penetrates.
The beam that sizzles eye-skin red, glues
retina, refracts and illuminates
from prism. A prison, I know, isolates with purpose
thus *prism* is its synonym in this, each hue tortured out
so that a spectrum is possible to the naked human
eye, its rods and cones. Aunt Ruby lies in pieces
trapped, as the cliché goes, in the *prison of her body*
as it shrinks and feasts upon itself. There's her skin
looking celadon at its edges, her white mouth floating off
into the pillow near the raised arm's slug-colored pit. Not much
from which I can divulge those biblical texts she used
to torture me with as a girl, repeating, "Husband *and* child.
You can't have one, you must have two," thus making the duality
of love my greater and greater pressure. Pain *is* a threshold
that changes, she knows, and would have me bounce, like sunlight off
whale or apple skin, into the beholder's eye being forever
the appropriate Christian tone and hue. Particle and wave.
Nothing is a single moment, she instructs.
No private event lacks history.
So science threatens through veils of health in which
Ruby is our newest Bacon, testing limits of the world's sincerity.
"Must I really swallow a gallon of enamel?" she whispers.
I look through her, this prison of sickness turned prism
to see where light might pierce as knife might cut, when God
isolated the past so finally: a single gray beam.
"All together then?" she murmurs. "Good."
Then sinks into the fat white solid of her bed, hands yellow
as a Whistler wash. "I'm doing this for you."
Watches, during the hour, our stares, which concentrate
and divide her. Like light, we'll help erode the things we want
to illuminate. It is a kind of desire.

fire

You remember I should not remember this.
    How wind
whipped through my legs in a way I might now
    consider sexual;
then, invasive. Flannel-clutched, screwed into
    my too-small
nightdress, hurried outside into sets of hands
    like dishes.
Was it arson or accident? The night turned upside
    outwards,
snapped like silks on which the pattern of the world is printed.
    In extreme heat
everything looks further away. We passed damp
    clothes across
our mouths, watched the frustum of a neighbor's silo-
    like house sizzle
into morning. Being five then I should not now recall
    coughing black smoke,
the fact the roof sailed up suddenly like a dhow in a hot sea
    wind. But there
it is. What you tell me should not affect me does.
    The fact of arson
or accident explained and then dismissed
    does not
put the child at rest in bed, knowing the bed to be
    a final place
of rest. One tremblor of the earthquake still means
    earthquake,
and a rising bathroom tide would indicate flood.
    "Accident"

is our safest word. I bring this up two nights after the back door
        has been found
unshackled from its frame, hewed roughly in two
        by a stranger.
There is nothing lovely about a fire. There is nothing lovely
        about dying
shark-blue and swollen, buried by a world. The fact
        we are each
fifteen years older does not dismiss the child's fear of choking
        on a scarf-length
line of smoke, the taste of ashes in one's mouth. Parents:
        they found her
wrapped in a tooth and char layette when they scraped her out.
        and somewhere
below our beds at midnight, a young man stands counting
        our radios
and change. No universe should care so much about our souls.
        But science's
statistics bespeak our own. We know heat seeks heat and fire
        goes back to fire.
And maybe crime fuels crime because it's energy, and to keep
        this world in motion
we must have it. Forget safety. Tell me more about accident.
        What I recall
is not the splintered door or scorched lot but the fact the universe
        gave me you.
Accidents fuel accidents that are blessings, too.
        What you don't
remember I do. That night in question—its arson, its accident—
        it was the first moment
I knew how to love you.

making out in korean

Are you here alone? Because Earth tilts and thus
         winter wears its same face yearly in a sky

distinct from summer's and, in 1998,
         you are reading, Saturday, 10 A.M.

the Thursday paper you've put off; so *Did you come alone?*
         no translation guides the shy consigned

to the black hole each party becomes.
         Because there are people whose single

world consists of gray but for whom "gray"
         has no meaning because *Your breasts are*

beautiful in their retrospectives of light, dark—the changeable
         shadings cast immutable in a brain's conal glows;

just as "snow" means everything and nothing to those
         obsessed with its surfaces and loving you,

stranger, has a vocabulary both abstract and distinct
         to this beige room, this street corner where

Oh, I'm so embarrassed I wear a dress
         the growl of neon; so

I have all the colorful phrases of the world generally used
         to turn to your specific. The cars here are blue.

They've covered the streets with vegetables. And
   though *Your eyes are stunning*

this time, believe me, *It's the truth* because isn't
   each season winter and every street

blue with cars and cabbages? Aren't all kitchens
   sewn like Thebes with plastic cups and phone numbers?

Tell me the truth. Isn't it summer now
   in Australia and the real world monochrome,

not variegated? I think of you in your white clothes others
   term "gray," the expectation that makes my eyes

call your eyes "brown."
   I am learning to associate with steel wool.

Because every day someone drowns
   learning to swim while the rest of us must

reinvent the word or memorize
   forgotten hues of fruit, so

I'm star-gazing these configured signs as clues
   to your desire till "Kim's Appliances"

becomes *I want to suck your boots*
   Berlitzed to commonplace "I love you."

Wanting you means wanting to inhale a universe.
   I'm here on this street corner telling you

a thousand ways *Marry me* how winter feels in a mouth
      devoid of seasons; now, the taste of oranges.

Tomorrow, you're out alone as usual, shopping
      for vegetables. I'm out too, 1998,

walking in my favorite public garden at night
      because I fear the color day calls "grass."

Listen, I'm telling you someone in the Ganges just pulled
      his first successful backstroke. It is summer

in Australia, dawn in Maine. *Don't give up on me.* I'm really alive
      in this linoleum eternity, diffident as a math problem

desperate to be solved. Right now I'm saying *I'm coming back.*
      I'm saying *Here,* I'm saying *Soon.* Listen: I'm telling you

Wait for me.

The Contemporary Poetry Series   EDITED BY PAUL ZIMMER

The Contemporary Poetry Series   EDITED BY BIN RAMKE

Patrick Lawler, *A Drowning Man Is Never Tall Enough*
Sydney Lea, *No Sign*
Jeanne Lebow, *The Outlaw James Copeland and the Champion-Belted Empress*
Phillis Levin, *Temples and Fields*
Gary Margolis, *Falling Awake*
Mark McMorris, *The Black Reeds*
Jacqueline Osherow, *Conversations with Survivors*
Jacqueline Osherow, *Looking for Angels in New York*
Tracy Philpot, *Incorrect Distances*
Paisley Rekdal, *A Crash of Rhinos*
Donald Revell, *The Gaza of Winter*
Martha Ronk, *Desire in L.A.*
Martha Ronk, *Eyetrouble*
Peter Sacks, *O Wheel*
Aleda Shirley, *Chinese Architecture*
Pamela Stewart, *The Red Window*
Susan Stewart, *The Hive*
Terese Svoboda, *All Aberration*
Terese Svoboda, *Mere Mortals*
Lee Upton, *Approximate Darling*
Lee Upton, *Civilian Histories*
Arthur Vogelsang, *Twentieth Century Women*
Sidney Wade, *Empty Sleeves*
Marjorie Welish, *Casting Sequences*
Susan Wheeler, *Bag 'o' Diamonds*
C. D. Wright, *String Light*
Katayoon Zandvakili, *Deer Table Legs*